ROBOTS AT WORK

WORLD BOOK

www.worldbook.com

Co-published by agreement between Shi Tu Hui and World Book, Inc.

Shi Tu Hui
Room 1807, Block 1,
#3 West Dawang Road
Chaoyang District, Beijing 100025
P.R. China

World Book, Inc.
180 North LaSalle Street
Suite 900
Chicago, Illinois 60601
USA

© 2026. All rights reserved. This volume may not be reproduced in whole or in part in any form without prior written permission from the publisher.

WORLD BOOK and the GLOBE DEVICE are registered trademarks or trademarks of World Book, Inc.

Library of Congress Control Number: 2025938162

Robots
ISBN: 978-0-7166-5814-6 (set, hard cover)

Robots at Work
ISBN: 978-0-7166-5819-1 (hard cover)

Also available as:
ISBN: 978-0-7166-5829-0 (soft cover)
ISBN: 978-0-7166-5839-9 (e-book)

WORLD BOOK STAFF

Writer: William D. Adams

Editorial

Vice President
Tom Evans

Senior Manager, New Content
Jeff De La Rosa

Associate Manager, New Content
William D. Adams

Content Creator
Elizabeth Huyck

Proofreader
Nathalie Strassheim

Graphics and Design

Senior Visual Communications Designer
Melanie Bender

Photo Editor
Rosalia Bledsoe

ACKNOWLEDGMENTS

Cover: © 35lab/Shutterstock; © Volvo Trucks; © Alexander Tolstykh, Shutterstock; © AKKA Technologies
4-5   © Noppawat Tom Charoensinphon, Getty Images; © Praphan Jampala, Shutterstock
6-7   © Josep Curto, Shutterstock
8-9   National Institute of Standards and Technology; © Gamma-Keystone/Getty Images
10-11   © FANUC; © Andrei Kholmov, Shutterstock
12-13   © Tecnowey
14-15   Public Domain; Hirata Robotics GmbH (licensed under CC BY-SA 3.0 DE)
16-17   Humanrobo (licensed under CC BY-SA 3.0)
18-19   © Ndoeljindoel/Shutterstock
20-21   © Alexander Tolstykh, Shutterstock
22-23   © Rethink Robotics
24-25   AGV Expert JS (licensed under CC BY-SA 3.0); Carmenter (licensed under CC BY-SA 4.0)
26-27   © Nataliya Hora, Shutterstock
28-29   © Tomas Westermark, Boliden; © Christian Sprogoe Photography/Rio Tinto
30-31   © Caterpillar
32-33   © CNH Industrial America; © Ruslan Ivantsov, Shutterstock
34-37   © Agrobot
38-39   © Aurora Innovation Inc.; © Volvo Trucks
40-41   Charles Buynak, U.S. Air Force; Doug Thaler (licensed under CC BY-SA 4.0)
42-43   © AKKA Technologies
44-45   © FBR Ltd
46-47   © Ted Hsu, Alamy Images

Contents

- **4** Dull, Dirty, Dangerous
- **6** Industrial Robots
- **8** HELLO, MY NAME IS: Unimate
- **10** Articulated Robots (Robotic Arms)
- **12** Cartesian and Gantry Robots
- **14** SCARA
- **16** Parallel Link Robots
- **18** ROBOT CHALLENGE: Working With People
- **20** HELLO, MY NAME IS: FANUC's lights-out factories
- **22** Cobots
- **24** Cart and Carry
- **26** Robot Risk: Technological Unemployment
- **28** Mining Robots
- **30** HELLO, MY NAME IS: Caterpillar 797F self-driving dump truck
- **32** Robotic Farming
- **34** HELLO, MY NAME IS: Agrobot Bug Vacuum
- **36** Automated Fruit Harvesting
- **38** Self-Driving Trucks
- **40** Inspection Robots
- **42** HELLO, MY NAME IS: Air-Cobot
- **44** Robot Construction
- **46** Hands-On Robotics
- **48** Glossary and Index

Terms defined in the glossary are in type **that looks like this** on their first appearance on any spread (two facing pages).

Dull, Dirty, Dangerous

Imagine if you worked on an assembly line and had to put the same two parts together over and over again. Or imagine you had to work in a dusty mine where rock falls were common. That doesn't sound too great, right? Fortunately, robots do many of these jobs for us. And with today's advances in robotics technology, they are poised to do even more.

Robots have been put to work in dull, dirty, and dangerous jobs. Robots are great at putting the same two pieces together in an assembly line, over and over, day after day. They can do jobs that people find gross, or that are in conditions that might make them sick. They can also be sent into areas that are too expensive—or

Dull duties
Does stamping the date on thousands of tuna cans sound like your dream job? Probably not! Robots do not mind such boring tasks, and they can do them quickly with few mistakes.

impossible—to make safe for humans. As robotics technology improves, robots are also being entrusted with delicate tasks that require more control than human hands can provide.

In this book, you will read about robots that work for people. You'll learn about the different types of **industrial robots.** You'll also get to meet some of the hard-working 'bots that help us people do some of the dullest and dirtiest, and most dangerous and delicate jobs.

Dangerous work
Robots can do such jobs as welding that carry a risk of injury, keeping human workers at a safe distance.

Industrial Robots

Industrial robots work in factories to help make many of the products we use every day. They come in many different shapes and sizes, but most stay bolted in one place. Work comes to them from conveyor devices.

Different industrial robots use different combinations of **rotary joints** and **translational joints.** In a rotary joint, one part twists or turns in relation to another, just like a human knee or wrist. In a translational joint, one part extends out or moves along a track. The angle between the two parts doesn't change, but one part moves in or out (or up or down) in relation to the other part.

The area in which a robot can reach is called its **work envelope.** Most industrial robots have at least three joints so they can have a large, flexible work envelope.

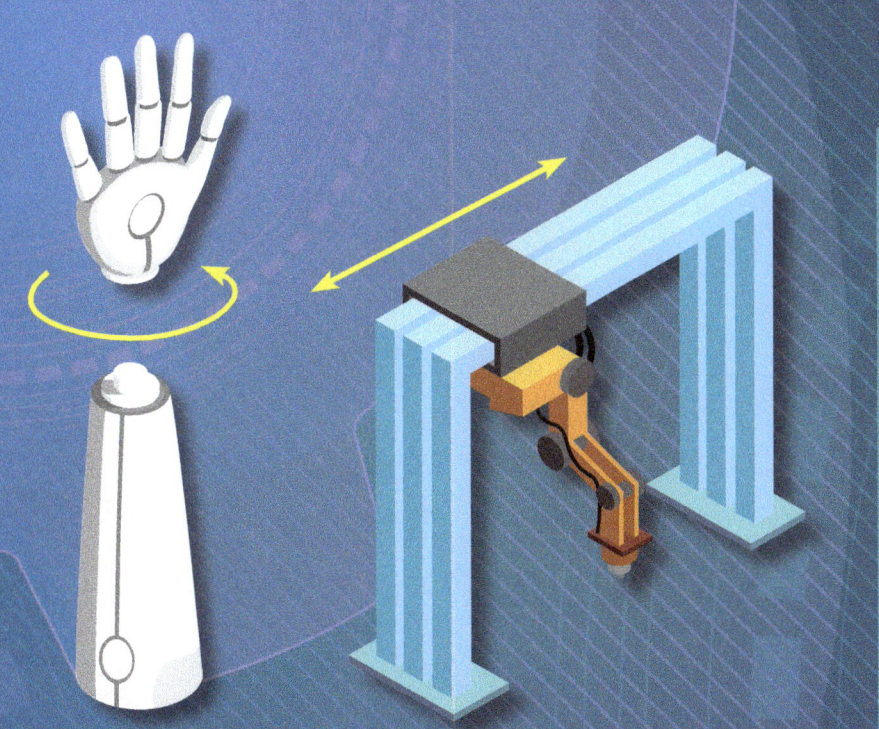

Work within reach
In a rotary joint (far left), one part twists in relation to another. In a translational joint (left), one part stretches out or moves along a track. Many robots have both kinds of joints (below).

HELLO, MY NAME IS:

Unimate

Unimate was the first **industrial robot.** It made its debut in 1961 at a U.S. automobile assembly plant. Unimate was a type of robot called a spherical robot. Its one **translational joint** and two **rotational joints** allowed it to reach within a circular **work envelope** around it. Today, most industrial robots are of other types.

Unimate was the first practical robot to gain media fame. It performed fun demonstrations for the public and made appearances on television.

AUTONOMY
MEDIUM

Robots are driven by more powerful computers today, enabling greater autonomy, but at the time, Unimate was a major breakthrough.

GOOD CO-WORKER

Though industrial robots took time to catch on, factory managers—and even the workers—where they were installed quickly grew to appreciate them. Unimation avoided selling to companies that were laying off employees to avoid resentment from other workers.

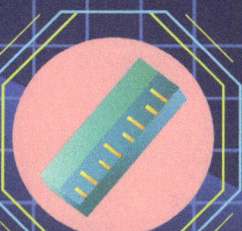
SIZE

Unimate was a hefty 'bot, weighing 2,700 pounds (1,200 kilograms).

MAKER

The American company Unimation created Unimate.

Articulated Robots (Robotic Arms)

Articulated robots are the workhorses of the **industrial robot** world. They usually have three or more **rotary joints,** creating a large, three-dimensional **work envelope** in which they can reach things to do their jobs.

Articulated robots come in all shapes and sizes. They can be fitted with different **actuators** to

Armed and ready An articulated robot is a robotic "arm" that can bend, twist, and reach to do its job.

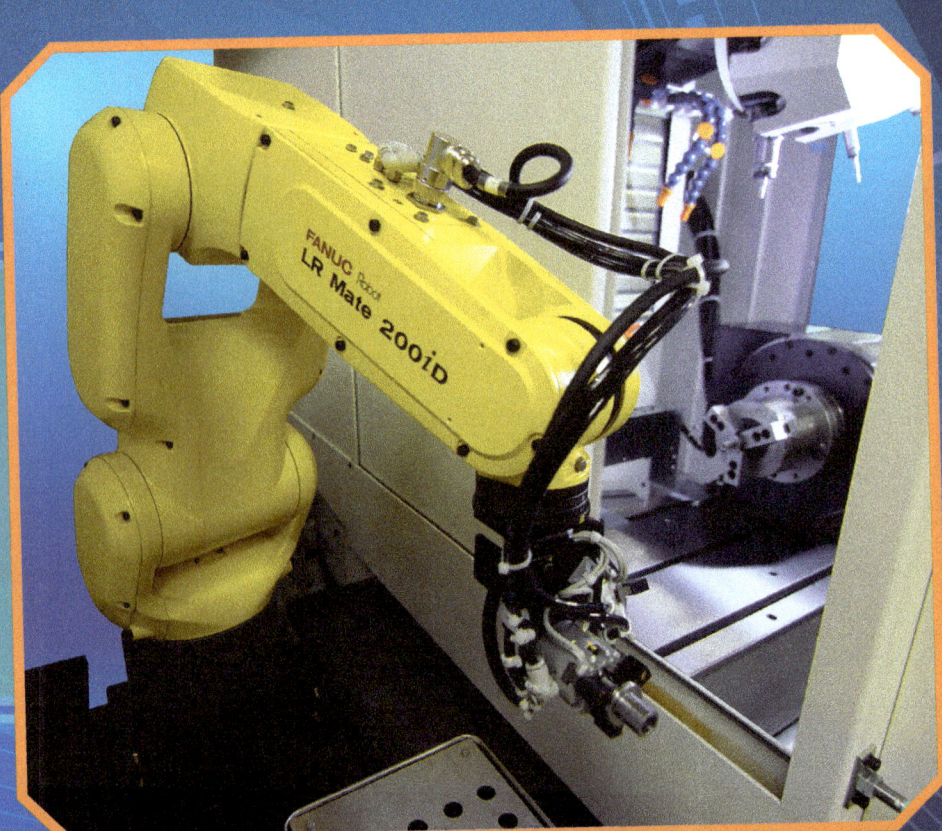

[10]

Articulated robots are used for all kinds of jobs. These articulated robots are painting cars.

do many different industrial tasks. They weld, move things, grind metal, or put parts together. Some even work with food!

Some articulated robots take manufactured goods and pack them onto pallets for easy shipment. A lot of material is moved on standard shipping pallets, which are 48 inches by 40 inches (122 centimeters by 102 centimeters).

Cartesian and Gantry Robots

Think of a claw crane game, where the claw can travel front-to-back, side-to-side, and finally down to try to grab a prize. Some **industrial robots** work much the same way. They have three **translational joints,** and sometimes work overhead. Fortunately for the factories that use them, their **effectors** are much more reliable than the claws of claw crane games!

Cartesian robots have three translational joints, all at 90-degree angles from one another, that allow parts of the robot to slide on a track. These robots are simple and effective, but their design allows them only to pick up smaller objects.

A gantry robot is similar to a Cartesian robot, but with an additional track over one or both horizontal axes to support the robot's weight. This arrangement allows for fine-tuned movements and larger loads. Gantry robots are often large and mounted high above the factory floor.

Gantry robots are like robotic cranes. In this warehouse, a gantry robot (shown at the top of the photograph) is used to stack containers.

SCARA

Circuit boards are computer components that are used in many modern machines, including robots. As the need for circuit boards exploded and the boards themselves got smaller and smaller, manufacturers needed ways to speed up production.

One solution is to assemble the boards with a kind of **industrial robot** called

Sketchy SCARA
SCARA robots are known for their pinpoint control. This 'bot fancies itself a bit of an artist.

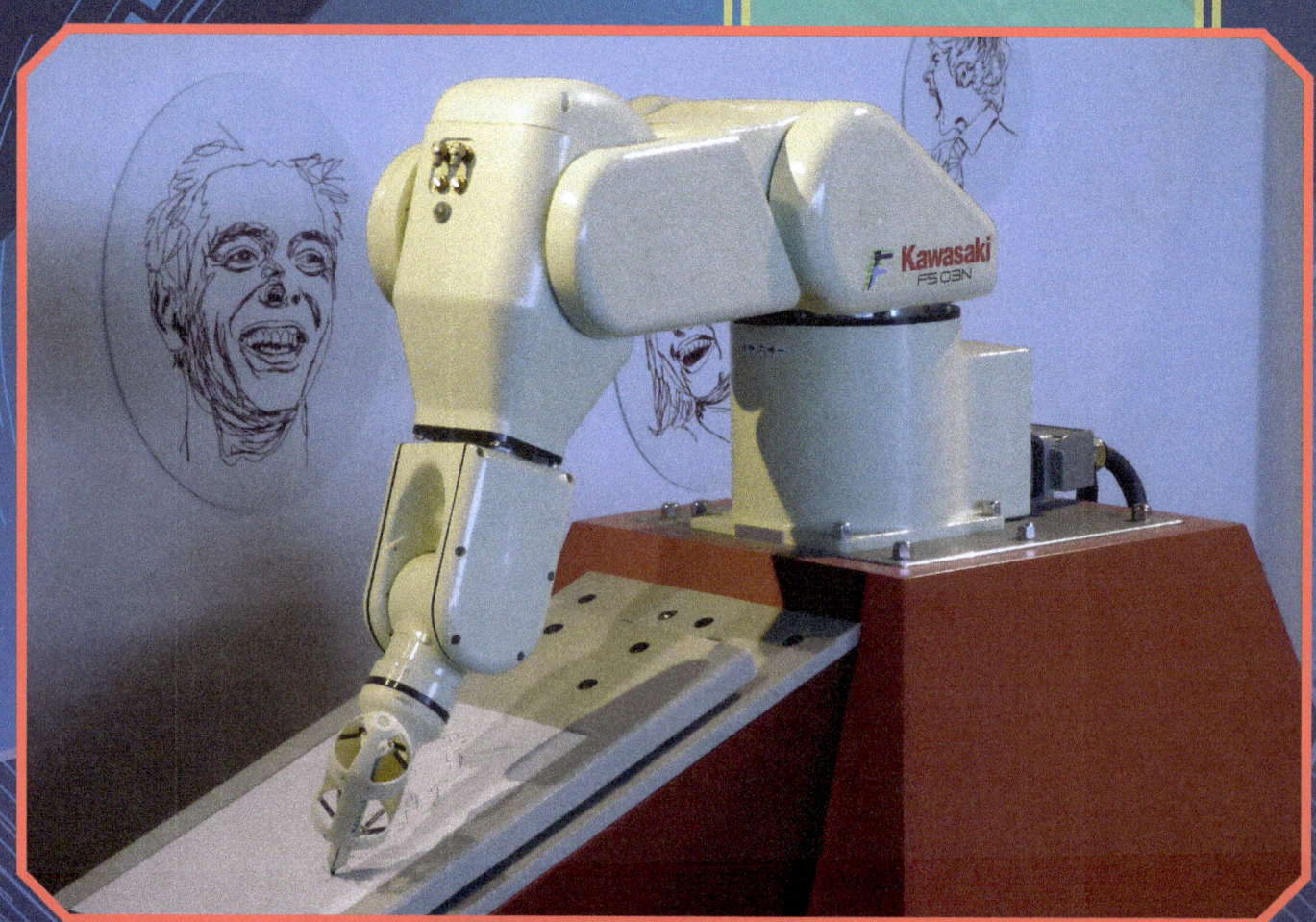

a *s*elective *c*ompliance *a*ssembly *r*obot arm (SCARA). SCARA's have two **rotary joints** that rotate on the same axis and one **translational joint** that raises and lowers the **effector**. This gives them a flatter **work envelope** than other types of industrial robots. But SCARA's have pinpoint control over this area, making them perfect for assembling circuit boards.

SCARA's are great for tasks that require only limited motions, such as packaging or handling small items.

[15]

Parallel Link Robots

Parallel link robots are a strange-looking type of **industrial robot.** Three or four arms, each with a **rotational joint actuator** at the base, all attach to a single **effector.**

Because the arms are attached together this way, the robot has a small **work envelope.** Why attach the arms together? Parallel link robots can move small items inside their work envelopes with amazing speed and precision. For example, they can take objects scattered on a conveyor belt and stack them neatly for packaging. While moving the objects, they can rotate them so that they are all facing the same direction.

Parallels link robots can sort and stack parts at lightning speed.

Industrial robots can be dangerous coworkers. They operate with a lot of force and don't always have sensors for what's around them. A person wandering into an industrial robot's **work envelope** could get clobbered by its swinging arm. Engineers have come up with different solutions to keep workers safe. Robots are often put in cages, not to keep the 'bots in, but to keep people from getting too close to them while they are working.

Be safe
Human workers use caution and wear safety equipment near an industrial robot.

Most robots also have a training mode, where the motors operate more slowly and with less power. This allows human programmers to enter a robot's cage to see if it's performing a new routine correctly.

HELLO, MY NAME IS:

FANUC's lights-out factories

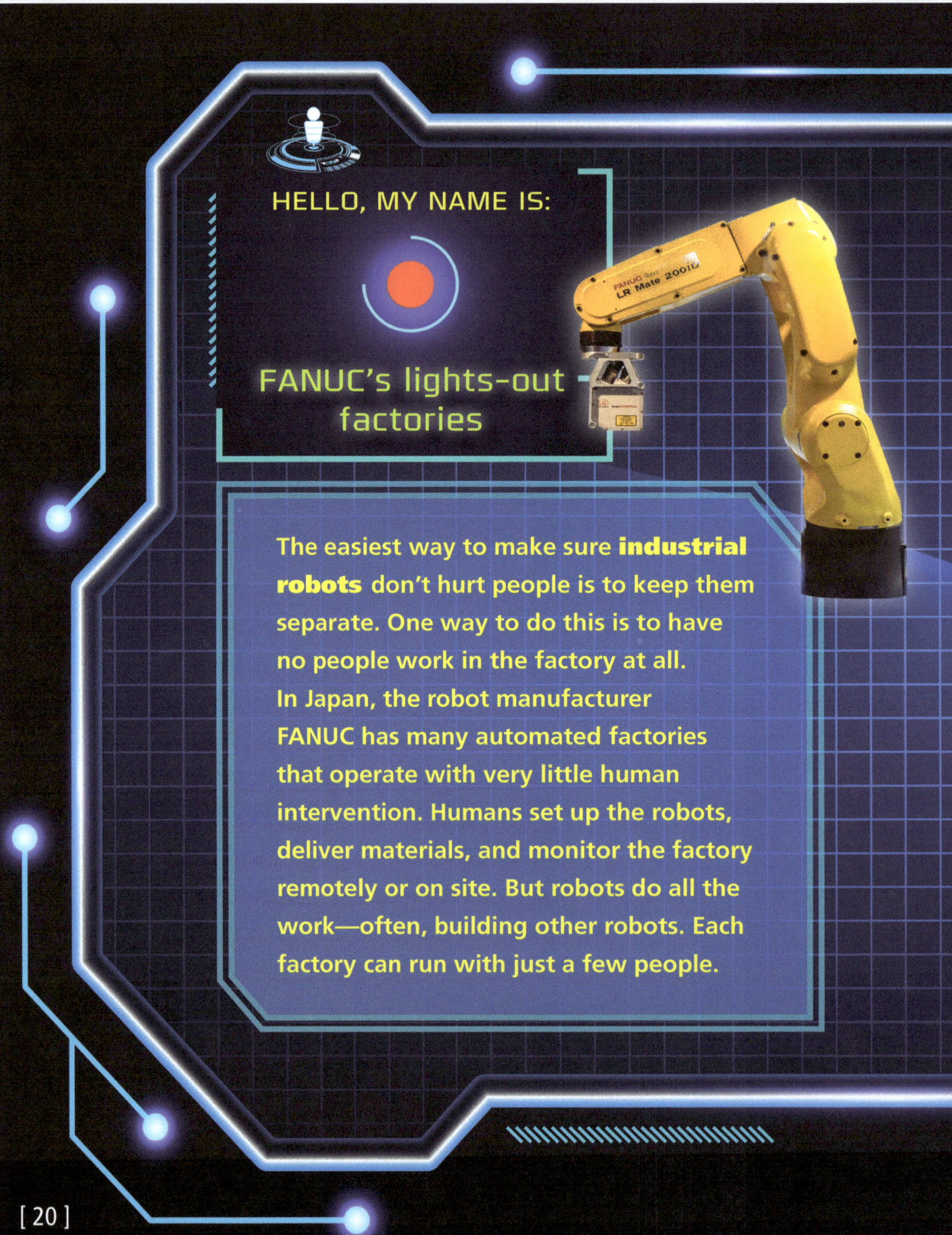

The easiest way to make sure **industrial robots** don't hurt people is to keep them separate. One way to do this is to have no people work in the factory at all. In Japan, the robot manufacturer FANUC has many automated factories that operate with very little human intervention. Humans set up the robots, deliver materials, and monitor the factory remotely or on site. But robots do all the work—often, building other robots. Each factory can run with just a few people.

AUTONOMY
`HIGH`

About 80% of the manufacturing process is completed by machines. Engineers do the wiring. The factories can go for up to 30 days without human input. People deliver raw materials to them. The robotic factories work until they run out of raw materials or space to store the new robots.

PRODUCTION
Over 2,000 robots can produce more than 100,000 robots every year. In 2023, Fanuc shipped their millionth robot.

MAKER
Japanese company FANUC

LIGHTS OUT
FANUC's factories rarely have people in them, so the lights are turned off to save energy. The robots work in the dark!

Cobots

Industrial robot manufacturers are also creating robots that are better coworkers. These **collaborative robots,** also known as **cobots,** have **sensors** to spot humans. Cobots are programmed to slow down, stop, or change their movement when people are near. More than that, cobots are designed to work with humans. Humans

Better together
Cobots are robots designed to work well with humans. Sawyer was an early cobot built by the American company Rethink Robotics. It featured video-screen eyes to show where its attention was focused.

[22]

Helping handoff
In this factory, Sawyer inspects the work of a human coworker before loading the part into a robotic welding machine.

even train some of them to perform tasks by guiding them through the movements needed to complete the task. Sensors and programmable **AI** help make cobots safer and more flexible for helping human workers with a variety of tasks. Cobots now work alongside people in many factories and small businesses, doing the difficult, repetitive, or boring parts.

[23]

Cart and Carry

Self-driving **automated guided vehicles (AGV's)** and **autonomous mobile robots (AMR's)** move things around factories and warehouses. Towing vehicles—also called tuggers—can push or pull carts loaded with pallets or raw materials to different locations. They can be many cars long and haul tens of thousands of pounds or kilograms.

Automated forklifts work just like their crewed counterparts. They slide long metal forks under a pallet packed with merchandise to pick it up and move it to a different location, guided by a program or following a set path. Robots also help stack shelves and unload trucks.

Tuggers (robotic towing vehicles) haul materials and products around factories and warehouses.

Automated forklifts lift pallets and shelve products.

ROBOT RISK
Technological Unemployment

Are robots getting too good at our jobs? Some people worry that improvements in robotics, **automation,** and **artificial intelligence (AI)** will put many people out of work. For instance, if self-driving car technology is perfected, fleets of **autonomous** taxis would put cab drivers and independent repair shops out of business.

Some jobs (such as car painter) have already been replaced by automation. But many jobs have parts that can't be automated easily. Robots and AI might do the boring parts of a job while people do the parts that require greater flexibility. Aided by robots and automation, the same number of people can do more work. Robots might allow a wider range of workers to do jobs that used to require physical strength. And there will be plenty of work for robot engineers, programmers, and mechanics.

Humans need not apply Human workers are nowhere to be seen in this photograph of a factory where jobs are done by robots.

Mining Robots

Mining is perfectly suited to robotic **automation:** it's often dull, dirty, and dangerous all at once. Add to that another D: distant. Many mines are far from where people live. People who work in these mines often have to live on-site, which is boring for them and expensive for the company. Automating mining processes means that fewer people have to be transported to or live at the mine site.

Robot miner
An automated loader scoops rock at a mine.

Loaded up and truckin' Huge robotic dump trucks haul rock and ore at a quarry. Mines, quarries, and similar sites have little traffic and few pedestrians, making it easy for autonomous vehicles to rule the road.

For aboveground mines, robots can use **Global Positioning System (GPS)** to find where they are. But GPS doesn't work underground, and many electronic **sensors** can't survive the harsh conditions found in underground mines. Some inventors are using rugged cameras combined with **software** that mimics the way nocturnal animals find their way around to create robots that can **autonomously** navigate underground mines.

Valuable minerals can be found in locations even more remote than faraway underground mines, such as the bottom of the ocean and asteroids in space. If mining could be completely automated, such sites might become profitable to mine.

[29]

HELLO, MY NAME IS:

Caterpillar 797F self-driving dump truck

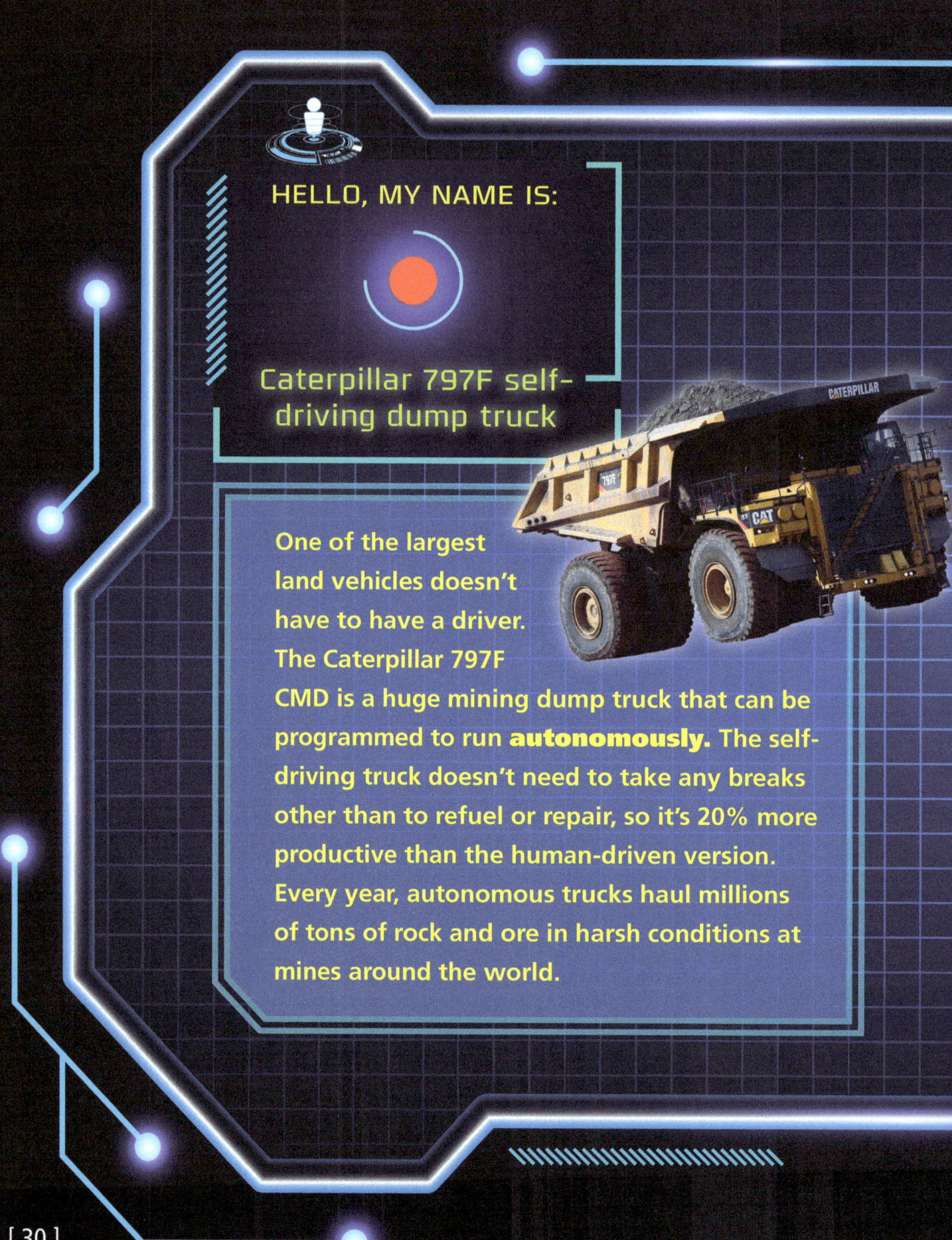

One of the largest land vehicles doesn't have to have a driver. The Caterpillar 797F CMD is a huge mining dump truck that can be programmed to run **autonomously.** The self-driving truck doesn't need to take any breaks other than to refuel or repair, so it's 20% more productive than the human-driven version. Every year, autonomous trucks haul millions of tons of rock and ore in harsh conditions at mines around the world.

AUTONOMY

HIGH

This titanic truck will pull up next to the digging machines, drive away when its bed is full, and dump the material at a dump site, all while avoiding other trucks and people.

MAKER

The American company Caterpillar makes a wide variety of self-driving dump trucks. Their systems can even be fitted onto competitor's trucks!

SIZE

1,375,000 pounds (623,690 kilograms), 25 feet (7.6 meters) tall, 49 feet (15 meters) long

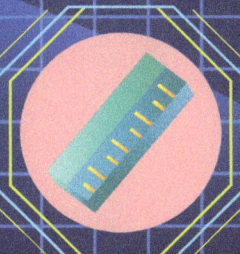

CAPACITY

400 tons (363 metric tons)—strong enough to carry two blue whales, the largest animal ever!

Robotic Farming

Many parts of farming are already **automated.** Beginning in the late 1990's, many tractors and combines have been fitted with **GPS** receivers, helping farmers to follow field plans with less effort. **Robotic vision** systems and other **sensors** help farm machines plow, plant, and harvest.

An easy row to hoe
Self-driving tractors allow a farmer to plant, fertilize, and harvest a field without ever setting foot in it.

Drone aircraft help farmers to keep an eye on huge fields of crops.

Now **artificial intelligence (AI)** is being harnessed to create fully driverless tractors and other equipment. Some farming tasks, such as harvesting, must be done in very short windows of time. Robotic farm equipment could work 24 hours a day if need be to get the job done.

Other farm robots can identify weeds and spray them with pesticide, or deliver fertilizer to just some plants. This uses less pesticide or fertilizer than whole-field spraying, reducing costs to the farmer and harm to the environment.

HELLO, MY NAME IS:

Agrobot Bug Vacuum

Fruit-munching bugs are pesky pests on fruit farms. Farmers want to get rid of bugs, but they also don't want to spray their fruit with poison. One solution is to suck up the bugs with a big vacuum! The Agrobot Bug Vacuum is a fully **autonomous** robot that patrols berry fields, sucking up bugs. **Lidar** and **robotic vision** detect crop rows, people, and other machines. The robot steers itself between rows and stops if it encounters an obstacle.

AUTONOMY

 HIGH

The Bug Vacuum can detect rows of plants and automatically steer itself through them, turning at the ends of rows.

WIND POWER

The Bug Vacuum holds two powerful vacuum canisters, which suck bugs off the plants and into a holding tank.

WIN-WIN-WIN

By controlling bugs without pesticides, the Bug Vacuum saves farmers money and means they lose fewer berries to bugs. It also reduces harm to the environment.

MAKER

The American company Agrobot makes the Bug Vacuum.

Automated Fruit Harvesting

Picking ripe fruit is more complicated than you might think. You have to identify fruit on a tree or bush, figure out whether it's ripe or not, and then gently pluck each fruit without damaging it or the plant. Humans get the hang of it pretty quickly, but it is a very difficult task for a robot to master.

Low-hanging fruit
A robot strawberry harvester does not touch the fruit. It simply grasps and cuts the long stem.

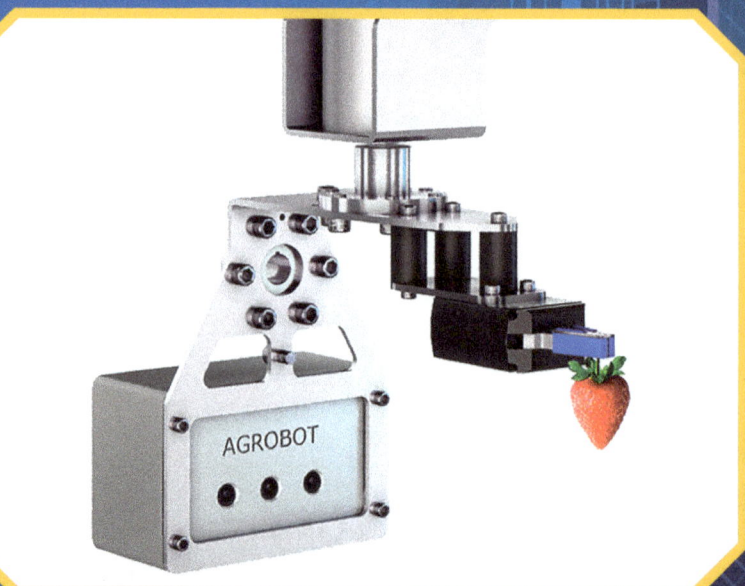

Agrobot E-Series pickers roll along over rows of strawberries, harvesting the fruit with robotic arms.

If this job is so hard for a robot to do, why are engineers trying to get robots to do it? Picking fruit is exhausting work. It needs to be done at certain times of year. It's hard to predict how many workers will be needed, and when they will be needed. Because of these difficulties, fruit sometimes rots before it can get picked.

New designs for fruit-picking robots use **artificial intelligence** systems to recognize ripe fruit and where to grasp it. Some designs use delicate grippers to grab the piece of fruit and pull it off the tree or bush. Others suck the fruit off with a vacuum.

Self-Driving Trucks

Long-haul trucking is a dull job. Most people who try it quit in their first year, so transportation companies have a hard time finding enough drivers. But someday soon, self-driving trucks could help share the load.

Self-driving trucks work in the same way as self-driving cars. An array of **lidar,** radar, and cameras mounted around the truck scan conditions, traffic, and the road. Powerful onboard computers steer, brake, and avoid collisions. Some self-driving trucks are already on the road in Texas, though they also carry a back-up human safety driver.

Aurora is an American company that makes a self-driving system that can be installed in any truck.

Autonomous trucks could have many advantages, especially on long stretches of highway. They can operate around the clock without stopping. Robot trucks never get tired or distracted, and never speed.

Navigating crowded city streets is more challenging. So autonomous trucks will probably travel between truck "hubs" outside cities. Human truckers would take over for the last stretch to stores, restaurants, and factories. Or trucks might be guided by remote control through city streets.

Self-driving short-hauler
The Swedish company Volvo is developing an electric, self-driving truck base called Vera. Vera is designed for short hauls, such as moving freight in a freight yard.

Inspection Robots

Some robots have important jobs, inspecting buildings, bridges, and other pieces of infrastructure. Small crawling robots or flying **drones** can check equipment in places humans cannot easily reach. They crawl along gas pipes, fly under bridges, climb electrical lines, and inspect inside ducts and sewers.

Inspector Snake Researchers test a snakelike inspection robot.

High-wire act
This remote-controlled inspection device climbs up and down bridge cables, looking for damage.

Some inspection 'bots are guided by remote control, with a human directing where they go. But many are **automated,** or fully **autonomous.** Someday soon, it may be normal to see small fleets of autonomous inspection drones buzzing around bridges, overpasses, and tunnels.

In many ways, robots are better inspectors than humans are. Once they are trained what to look for, they will almost always find it if it's there. With IR and UV cameras, they can detect cracks or imperfections too small for human eyes to see.

HELLO, MY NAME IS:

Air-Cobot

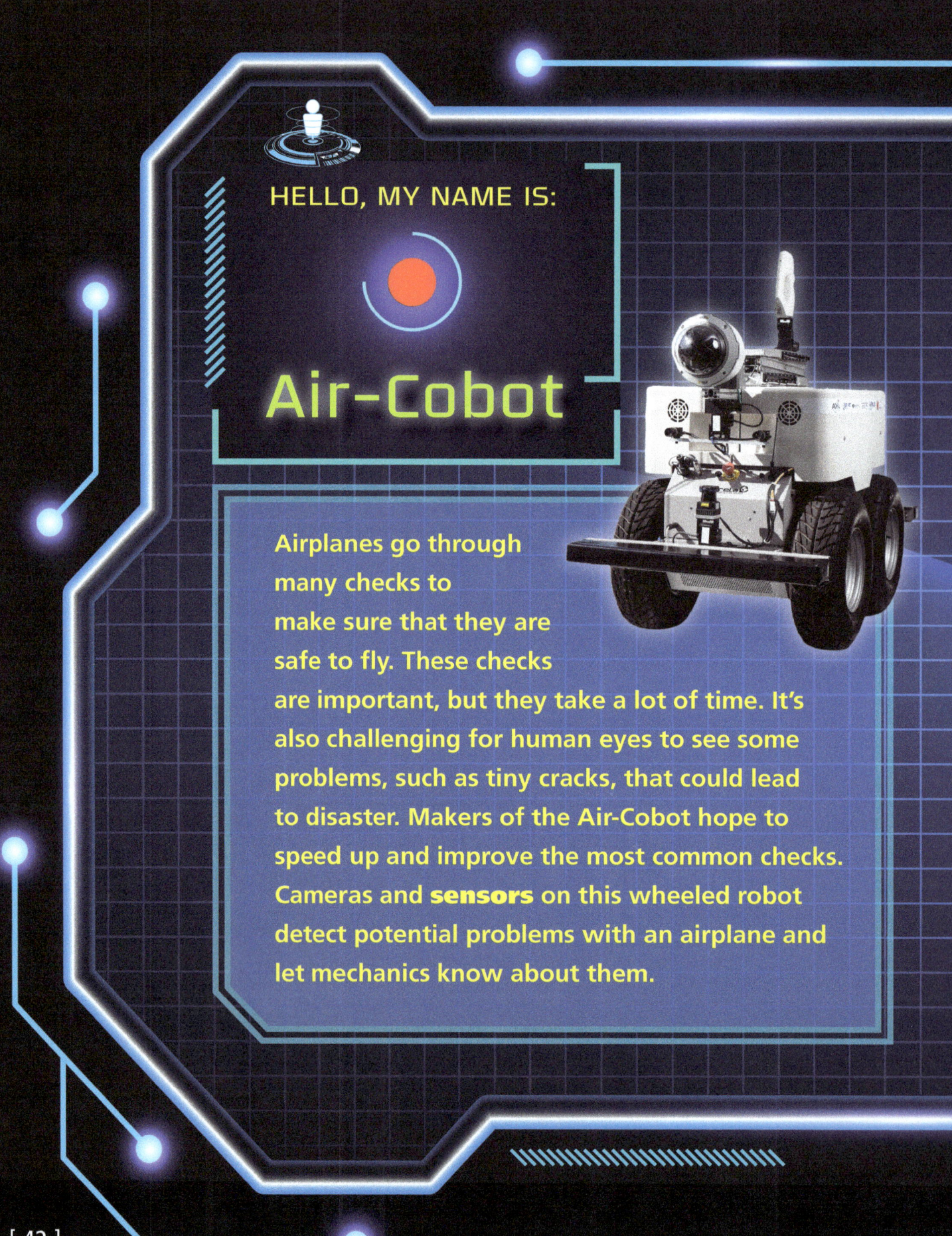

Airplanes go through many checks to make sure that they are safe to fly. These checks are important, but they take a lot of time. It's also challenging for human eyes to see some problems, such as tiny cracks, that could lead to disaster. Makers of the Air-Cobot hope to speed up and improve the most common checks. Cameras and **sensors** on this wheeled robot detect potential problems with an airplane and let mechanics know about them.

AUTONOMY
HIGH

Air-Cobot drives out to the planes to perform scheduled inspections. It will alert mechanics when it has found a problem with an airplane. When it is running low on power or needs maintenance, it returns to its hangar.

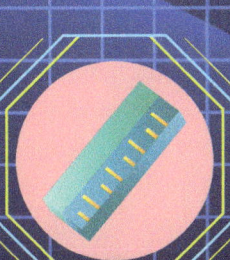

SIZE
57 x 31 x 47 inches (145 x 80 x 120 centimeters)

MAKER
A collaboration of five French companies, led by AKKA and Airbus, makes Air-Cobot.

WORKS WELL WITH OTHERS!
Air-Cobot is designed to work in busy airports. It has many sensors to avoid obstacles, such as luggage carts and workers, while performing or traveling to an inspection. Air-Cobots store their reports and images in a shared database, allowing them to compare damage and wear among planes. Air-Cobots partner with autonomous **drones** to check the upper parts of airplanes.

[43]

Robot Construction

After a hard day at work, it's nice to come home. Why not let a robot build one for you?

Brick-laying in the hot sun can be hard, tedious, and sometimes dangerous. Now a company in Australia has developed a robot that can lay bricks and concrete blocks. The robot looks like a truck with a huge arm. A computer inside directs the arm where to place each brick, following a detailed build plan. **Sensors** in the arm control where each brick goes and the force with which it is placed. Builder 'bots work quickly and precisely, putting together the frame of a house in as little as a few days.

Other construction robots work in factories, making modular units that get assembled into houses.

Brick by brick is how the HadrianX robot builds houses. AI software guides the robotic arm, following a computer-assisted design (CAD) plan of the building.

Hands-On Robotics

Want to get started making robots? Jump right in!

VEX Robotics

VEX believes that all kids are natural scientists and engineers. Their classroom kits and competitions are designed to inspire tinkering. In the VEX Robotics competitions, teams build robots from VEX kit parts to complete a group challenge and earn skill points in a timed trial.

Many teams come from schools, but not all. In competitions, two teams join up to compete against two other teams in a challenge course. Then each robot does a single timed trial. Competitions are held at local, regional, national, and international levels. Students from all over the world compete.

VEX has many different levels of robot kits and competitions.
• Younger kids can get stared with VEX GO.
• VEX IQ is for students in grades 4-8.
• VEX V5 Robotics competition is for grades 6-12.

VEX hopes to inspire kids to become robot builders for the future, to find new ways to put robots to work. What job will your robot have?

VEXed

Student-built VEX robots compete to collect balls and move them to a target area in a challenge competition.

Also check out:
- FIRST Robotics
- Best Robotics
- National Robotics Challenge (U.S.)

Or ask at your local school, library, or maker space.

Glossary

actuator a device, such as a motor, that provides movement to a robot.

articulated robot a robot that uses rotary joints. The most common articulated robots are armlike industrial robots.

artificial intelligence (AI) the ability of a computer system to process information in a manner similar to human thought or to exhibit humanlike behavior.

automation the use of machines to perform tasks that require decision making.

automated guided vehicle (AGV) a mobile robot that follows wires, tape, or markers to move items or people around.

autonomous mobile robot (AMR) a self-driving robot that does not need a defined path.

autonomy the degree to which a robot can make decisions without input from a human operator to achieve a goal.

collaborative robot (cobot) an industrial robot designed to work closely with people and share workspaces with them.

drone an uncrewed aerial vehicle. Most drones are piloted remotely, but some are autonomous.

effector the part of the robot's body, such as a wheel or a gripper, that is moved by an actuator and interacts with the environment to perform an action.

Global Positioning System (GPS) a worldwide navigation system that uses radio signals broadcast by satellites.

industrial robot a robot that works in a factory to help create a product.

lidar a sensor that uses beams of light to judge the distance of objects. The word *lidar* comes from *l*ight *d*etection *a*nd *r*anging.

robotic vision the use of cameras and computers to recognize patterns and objects in images.

rotary joint a type of joint in which one end rotates or twists in relation to the other.

sensor a device that takes in information from the outside world and translates it into code.

software a general term for computer programs. A computer program is mostly made up of a sequence of instructions. The instructions tell a computer what to do and how to do it.

translational joint a type of joint in which one part extends out or moves along a track.

work envelope the area in which an industrial robot can reach and manipulate objects with its effector.

Index

A
actuators, 10-11, 16
Agrobot (company), 34-37
Air-Cobot (robot), 42-43
airplane safety checks, 42-43
articulated robots, 10-11
artificial intelligence (AI), 26, 33, 37
automated guided vehicles (AGV's), 24
automation, 26, 28
automobiles: manufacturing, 8, 11; self-driving, 26. *See also* trucks, self-driving
autonomous mobile robots (AMR's), 24

B
berry farming, 34-37
Bug Vacuum (robot), 34-35

C
Cartesian robots, 12-13
Caterpillar 797F CMD dump truck, 30-31
circuit board production, 14-15
cobots, 22-23, 42-43
construction, 44-45

D
drone aircraft, autonomous, 33, 39, 40, 43
dump trucks, 28-31

E
effectors, 12, 15, 16

F
FANUC (company), 20-21
farming, 32-37
fertilizer, 33
forklifts, automated, 24-25
fruit harvesting, 36-37

G
gantry robots, 12-13
Global Positioning System (GPS), 29, 32, 35

H
HadrianX (robot), 44-45

I
industrial robots: first, 8-9; manufacturing, 20-21; safety and, 4-5, 18-21, 40-41; working with humans, 22-23
inspection robots, 40-41

J
joints. *See* rotary joints; translational joints

M
manufacturing: automobile, 8, 11; circuit board, 14-15; robot, 20-21
mining robots, 28-31

P
pallets, 11, 24-25
parallel link robots, 16-17
pesticide, 33, 35

R
Rethink Robotics (company), 22-23
robotic arms. *See* articulated robots
robotic vision, 32-34
rotary joints, 6-7, 8, 10, 15

S
safety, 4-5, 18-21, 40-41
Sawyer (robot), 22-23
SCARA robots, 14-15
sensors, 22, 29, 32, 35, 42, 43
software, 29

T
tractors, 32, 34
training modes, 19
translational joints, 6-7, 8, 12-13, 15
trucks, self-driving, 38-39; mining, 28-31
tuggers, 24

U
unemployment, 26-27
Unimate (robot), 8-9

V
Vera (truck), 39
VEX Robotics, 46-47
Volvo Trucks, 39

W
welding, 5
work envelope, 6, 8, 10, 15, 16; danger to workers in, 19

[48]

www.ingramcontent.com/pod-product-compliance
Lightning Source LLC
Chambersburg PA
CBHW061254170426
43191CB00041B/2424